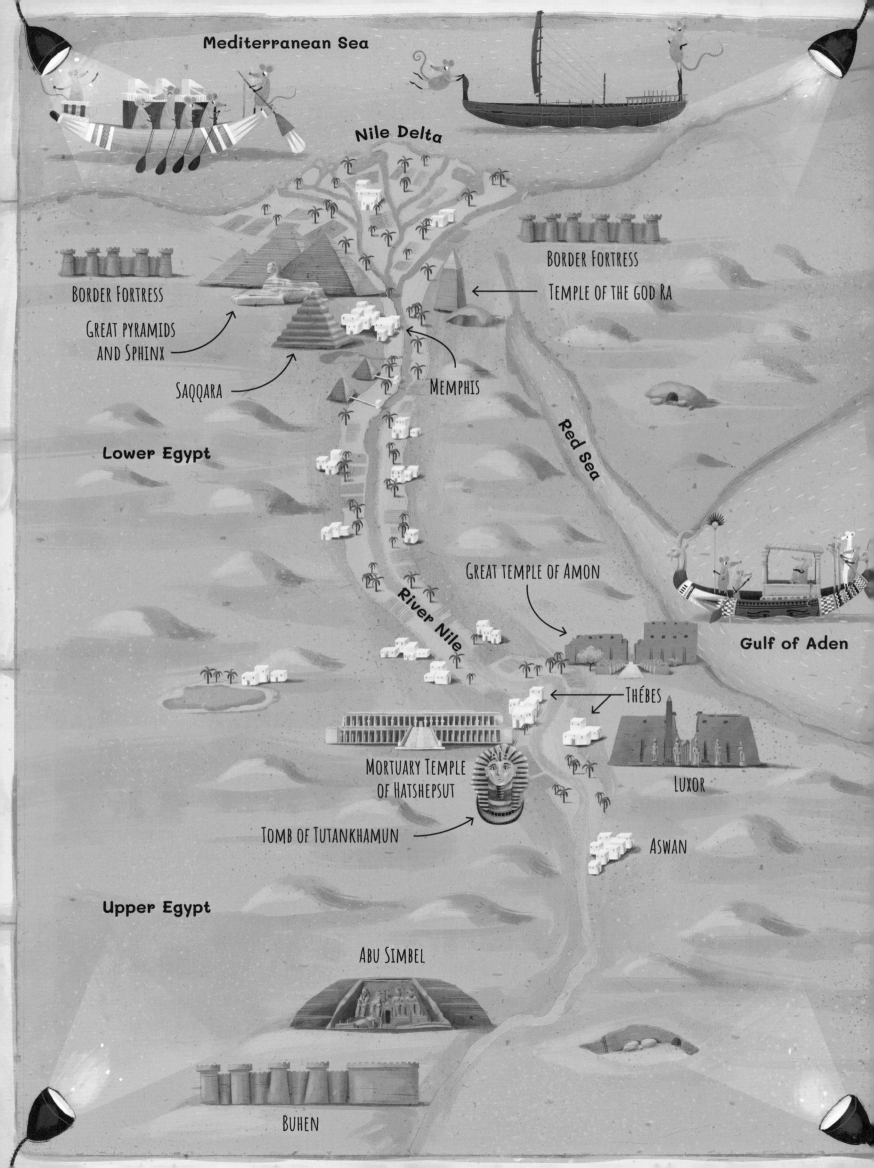

MAGICAL MUSEUM:

ANCIENT EGYPT

ANCIENT EGYPT is one of the oldest civilizations in the world. Dating back to 5000 BCE, it flourished around the mighty Nile River. Ancient Egyptians knew how important it was to live near this river. In the rainy season, the river would overflow its banks and flood the land, but when the waters receded, the land was enriched with fertile river sediment. That's why this area turned out to be ideal for growing crops. And that's why nomadic peoples began to settle permanently in the Nile Valley and farm the land, which gave them all the food they needed. This is how Ancient Egypt was born. In the beginning, it was divided into two separate realms: Upper Egypt, which lay in the river valley in the south, and Lower Egypt, which emerged around the Nile Delta in the north. The Nile wasn't only extraordinarily good for crops — over time, it became an important trade route for merchant ships, so important towns grew up on its banks. In 3000 BCE, the pharaoh Menes united Upper and Lower Egypt and founded the first dynasty, which was based in the capital Memphis. Thus began the history of Ancient Egypt under the reign of the pharaohs.

ENTER $\longrightarrow$

» TABLE OF CONTENTS «

Do you realize, dear reader, what you've done by opening this book? You've activated the curse of the sacred golden scarab, a symbol of rebirth for the Ancient Egyptians. Amulets with the image of this beetle were even placed on the hearts of mummies. Well, now you've brought this one back to life, and now it will awaken all of Egypt, thanks to the spell. Pharaohs, queens, nobles, and ordinary Egyptians will rise up and wonder what's happened to them. Oh dear, it's going to be a mess! How do we get out of this fix? Well, certainly not by closing the book. Leave it here in my paws. I'll simply run and catch the scarab to undo its spell. It might take some time, though. After all, meeeyyyaaawwwn . . . I've been out of action for quite a while — over 2,000 years, in fact! I could do with some help. Will you give me a hand? That's very kind of you. Welcome to the **MAGICAL MUSEUM** . . .

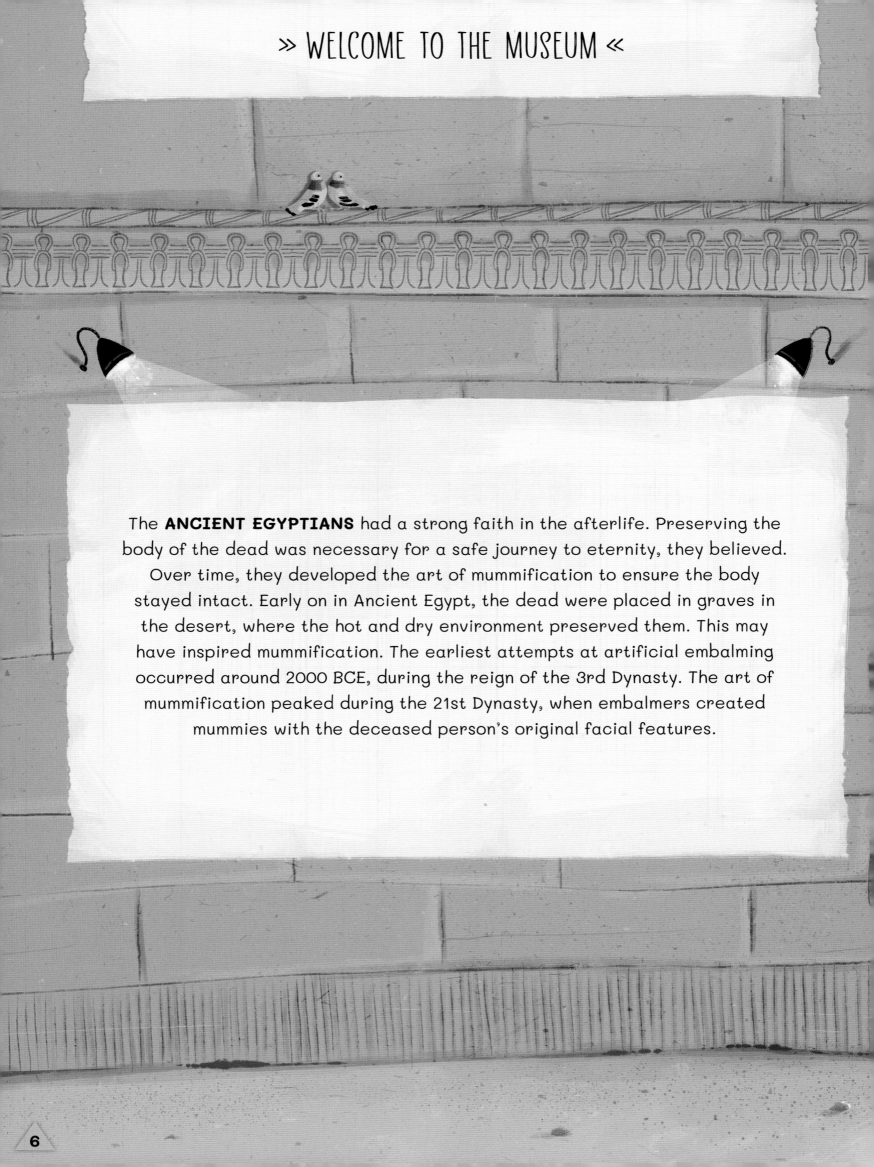

The **ANCIENT EGYPTIANS** had a strong faith in the afterlife. Preserving the body of the dead was necessary for a safe journey to eternity, they believed. Over time, they developed the art of mummification to ensure the body stayed intact. Early on in Ancient Egypt, the dead were placed in graves in the desert, where the hot and dry environment preserved them. This may have inspired mummification. The earliest attempts at artificial embalming occurred around 2000 BCE, during the reign of the 3rd Dynasty. The art of mummification peaked during the 21st Dynasty, when embalmers created mummies with the deceased person's original facial features.

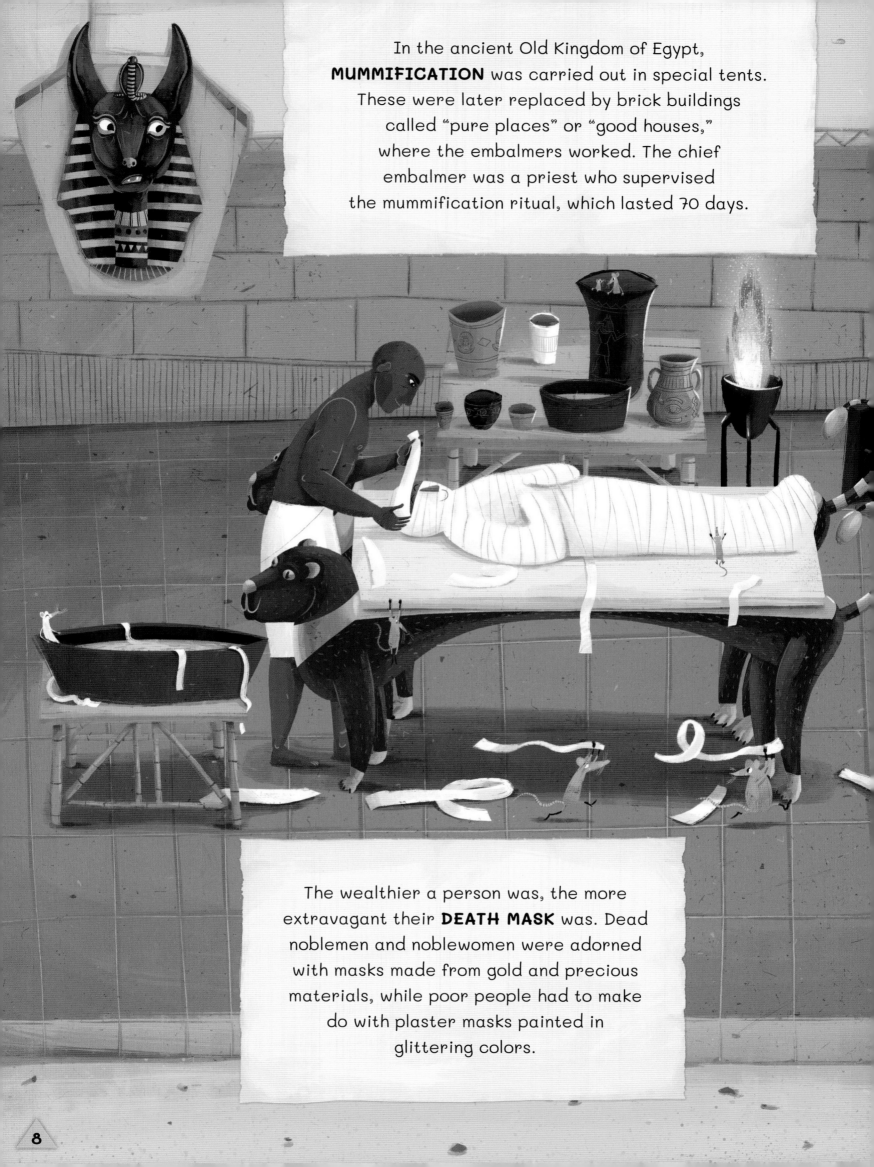

In the ancient Old Kingdom of Egypt, **MUMMIFICATION** was carried out in special tents. These were later replaced by brick buildings called "pure places" or "good houses," where the embalmers worked. The chief embalmer was a priest who supervised the mummification ritual, which lasted 70 days.

The wealthier a person was, the more extravagant their **DEATH MASK** was. Dead noblemen and noblewomen were adorned with masks made from gold and precious materials, while poor people had to make do with plaster masks painted in glittering colors.

Wow, I know this place! This is where they mummified me.

The **PRIESTS** in charge of the mummification provided tombs for poorer people, which they exchanged for money or material possessions. They also collected fees from the dead person's relatives for the upkeep of the mummy and the tomb, as well as all the spiritual services for 70 days. The journey into the afterlife didn't come cheap.

First, the embalmers took the brain and internal organs out of the body. Only the heart was left in the body, as the Egyptians considered it to be the center of a person's intelligence and feeling.

The removed liver, lungs, stomach, and intestines were washed in natron (a natural salt) and then stored in special containers called canopic jars.

They washed the body with palm wine, put natron inside it, and also sprinkled natron on the outside.

After 40 days, they filled the dried body with sawdust, leaves, straw, or cloth soaked in resin, smeared it with fragrant oils, and wrapped it in long strips of cloth. Between the layers of cloth, they put protective amulets.

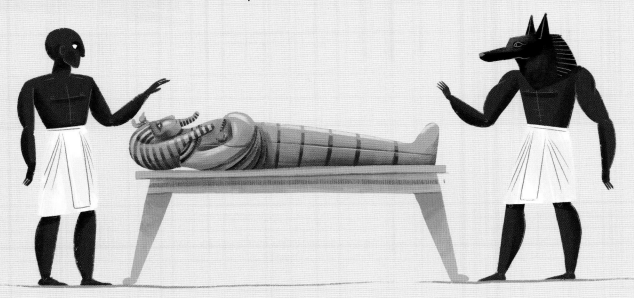

Lastly, the embalmers covered the body's head with a funeral mask and placed the body in a coffin. All the while, they would recite prayers for the soul of the deceased.

CANOPIC JARS, which held the internal organs of the deceased, had lids shaped like the heads of four deities. **Imset** (the one with the human head) watched over the liver. **Qebehsenuef** (with a falcon head) guarded the intestines. **Hapi** (with a baboon head) watched over the lungs. And **Duamutef** (with a jackal head) guarded the stomach.

In addition to the grave goods that the deceased was expected to use in the afterlife, they were also buried with **USHABTIS** — small figurines made of wood, stone, metal, ceramics, or glazed earthenware. These figurines were important servants who helped do manual labor in the afterlife.

1: **Hatshepsut** — A queen of the 18th Dynasty and one of the most important female Egyptian rulers. Ruling in place of her underage son Thutmose III from 1479—1458 BCE, she helped start new trade routes and grand construction projects.

2: **Thutmose II** — A pharaoh from the 18th Dynasty who ruled from 1493—1479 BCE. The wife of Thutmose II was the famous queen Hatshepsut.

3: **Seti I** — A pharaoh from the 19th Dynasty of the New Kingdom. He fortified the borders of Egypt, opened mines and quarries, and made the magnificent temple in Karnak. He reigned from 1290—1279 BCE.

4: **Ramesses II** — A pharaoh from the 19th Dynasty who reigned from 1279—1213 BCE. He brought prosperity to the empire during his long reign. He had a temple built in Abusir, a testament to his power and influence.

5: **Ahmose-Nefertari** — The first queen of the 18th Dynasty and wife of Pharaoh Ahmose I. She reigned from 1562—1495 BCE.

1 — **Pharaohs** were the highest-ranking members of Ancient Egyptian society. They had complete control of the empire, ensuring that laws were enforced and that all the wealth was kept in their hands. Common Egyptians viewed their pharaohs as gods, showing them respect and admiration. 2 — **Priests** were the second most important social class. Serving the gods, they offered up sacrifices and performed important rituals. Over time, they became more powerful than the pharaohs, even ruling over the whole Egyptian Empire for a while. 3 — **Officials** were the third tier of Egypt's social hierarchy. They taxed people and ran the justice system. The most powerful royal official was the vizier. Lower officials included scribes, who among other duties managed the royal storehouses of grain. 4 — **Military commanders and soldiers**, who protected the empire and expanded its territory through conquests, were the fourth level of the social pyramid. 5 — **Merchants and craftsmen. 6 — Peasants. 7 — Enslaved people and prisoners of war.**

Meow, I almost caught that bewitched little beetle. It's driving me crazy. Where has it gone now?

A **SARCOPHAGUS** was the final resting place of the dead. More than one sarcophagus is called sarcophagi, and they were often found along the western walls of burial chambers, surrounded by luxurious burial goods. The simplest ones were made of wicker or fired or unfired clay. The wealthy, however, were laid to rest in ornate coffins made from rare types of wood or stone.

1. Early Dynastic Period (3000—2686 BCE). Small oval- and square-shaped coffins made of wicker, fired clay, and unfired clay were the norm. Another option was for the deceased to be placed in round ceramic vessels.

2. Old Kingdom (2700—2181 BCE). Square-shaped sarcophagi made of alabaster, limestone, and granite were used. These walls were decorated with reliefs of palace façades and the names and titles of the deceased. Pharaohs were buried in large coffins made of cedar wood, while members

of the aristocracy were allowed the luxury of decorated wooden coffins.

3. Middle Kingdom (2055—1680 BCE). In this era, it was popular for royal sarcophagi to be made of stone, and as many as three coffins were placed in them. The coffin containing the body was gold, as was the mask worn by the deceased. By the end of the Middle Kingdom, coffins were shaped like the human body, doubling for the deceased's body if it got lost or damaged.

4. Second Intermediate Period (1650—1550 BCE). Coffins were typically carved from a single piece of wood. The lid of the coffin often featured a body wrapped in two wings, wearing an elaborate wig.

5. New Kingdom (1550—1069 BCE). Egyptian burial practices shifted, with two or three coffins being placed in a sarcophagus. The most frequently used materials for these were limestone, quartzite, and granite, and they were usually shaped like a cabinet or a human body.

» THE FAMOUS TOMB OF TUTANKHAMUN «

On November 26, 1922, in the Valley of the Kings, amateur archeologist **Howard Carter**, along with his patron Lord Carnarvon, stumbled upon a virtually undisturbed tomb. Little did they know it, but the tomb had lain untouched for a whopping three millennia. The tomb consisted of four rooms — an antechamber, an annex, a burial chamber, and a treasury — all overflowing with unbelievable riches. It took Carter eight years to gather all of the 3,500 valuables it contained.

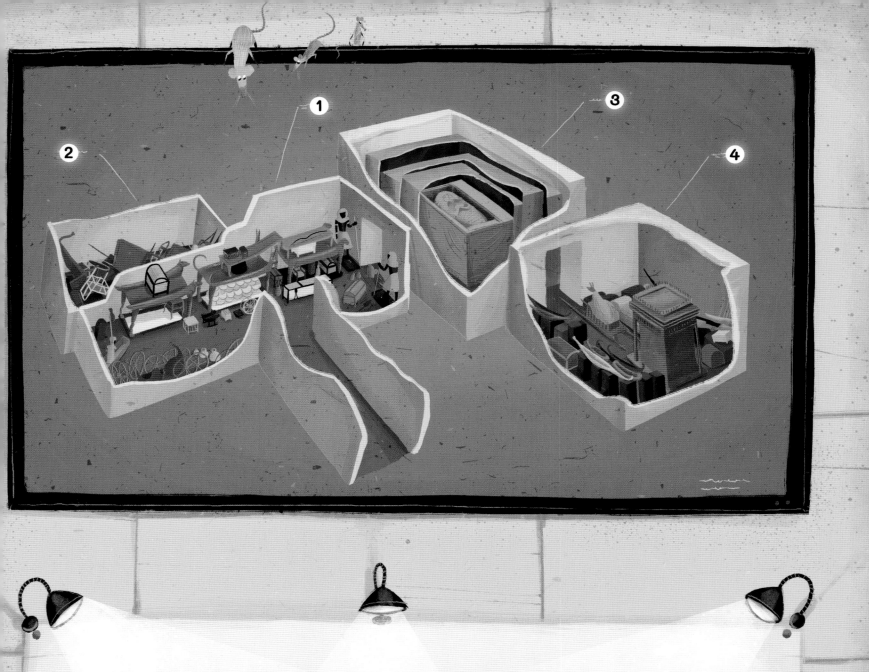

In the **antechamber ❶**, archeologists discovered chariots, funerary beds, Tutankhamun's legendary throne, and wooden and gilded statues. **The annex ❷** contained beds and chairs. In the **burial chamber ❸**, there were three nested coffins containing the body of the young Tutankhamun, richly decorated with jewels and amulets. Tutankhamun's coffin was made from over one ton of gold. The other two coffins were from wood covered with gold leaf. To this day, the most valuable find is Tutankhamun's beautiful gold death mask. In **the treasury ❹**, the archeologists were also surprised to find 30 model boats, several wooden cabinets filled with equipment for the afterlife, statues, and a canopic chest with the organs of the dead pharaoh.

Hey, kitty, kitty, kitty! I'm just dying to tell you about my life's crowning glory. It brought great fame to a hitherto unknown researcher and to an otherwise quite minor pharaoh.

I was filled with anxiety. I had only 14 days to uncover something great in the excavation - or else it would be shut down . . . Hey! Hold on! Where are you going? Leave that beetle alone and listen to me . . .

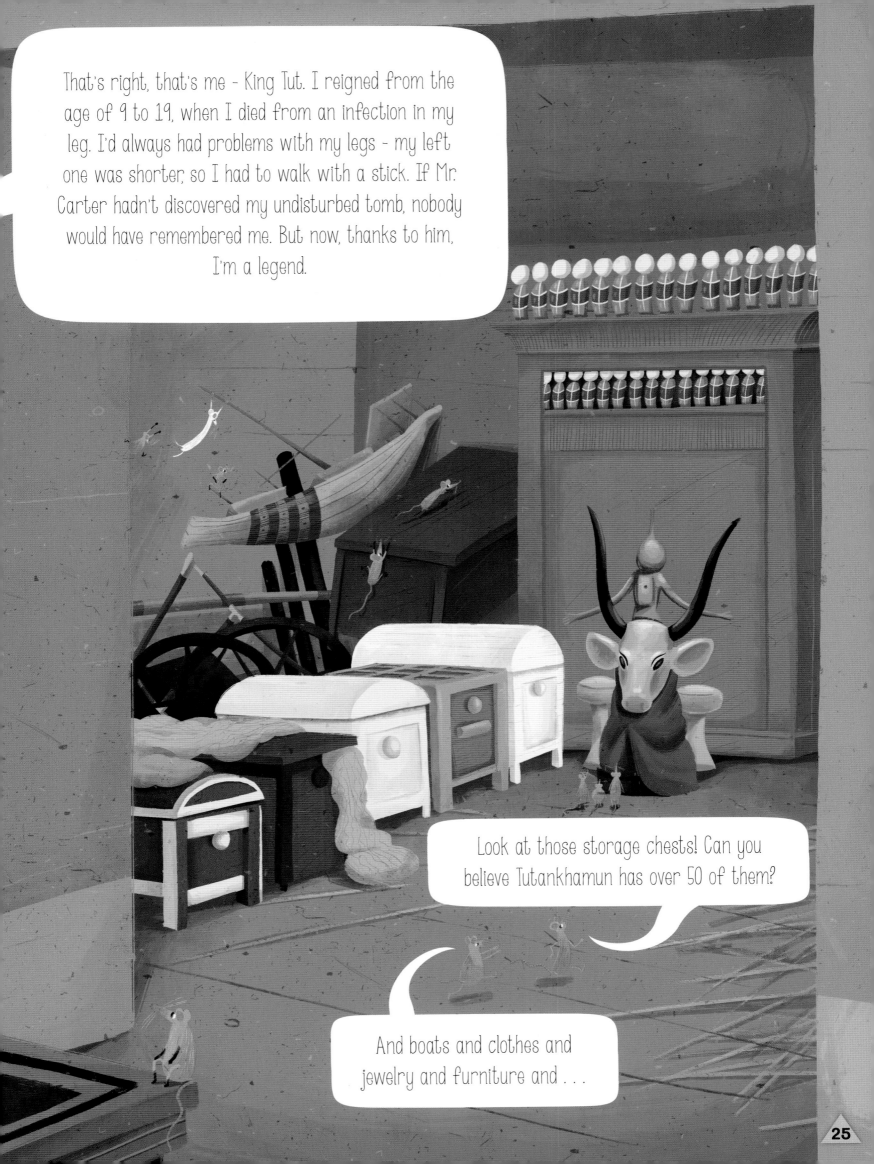

» PYRAMIDS AND TEMPLES «

The **PYRAMIDS** were made to be the final resting place of the pharaohs. The oldest Egyptian pyramid is the Step Pyramid of Djoser, which was built 5,000 years ago for Pharaoh Djoser. The renowned Egyptian architect and physician Imhotep was the person who had it built.

Yeah, I don't think I would want a little old mastaba either. I would want a huge pyramid all for myself!

Before the pyramids, pharaohs were laid to rest in tombs known as **MASTABAS**. However, Imhotep came up with the idea of building several mastabas on top of each other. Thus was born the first Egyptian pyramid. The most famous one is the **GREAT PYRAMID** of Giza, which belonged to the monarch Khufu (also known as Cheops) and was built around 2500—1500 BCE. It is 450 feet high and its walls face the four cardinal directions of north, south, east, and west.

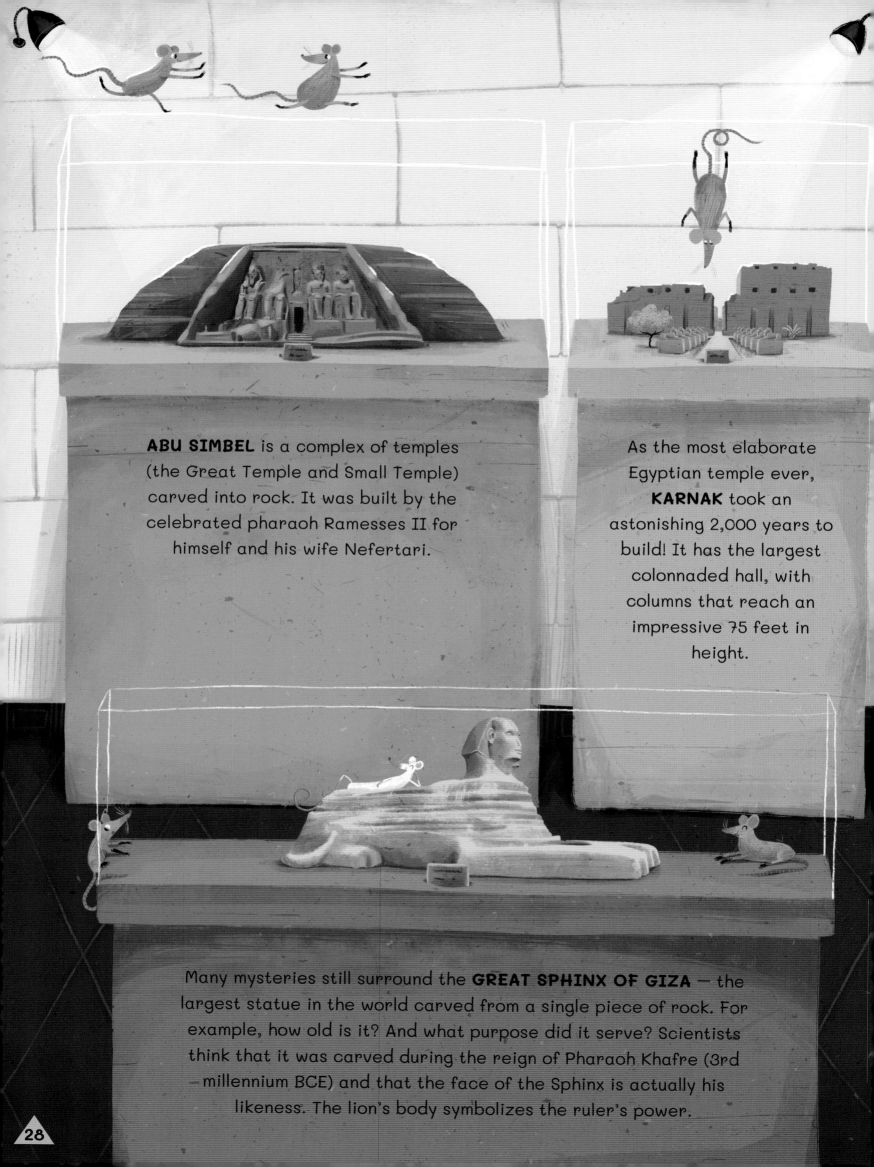

ABU SIMBEL is a complex of temples (the Great Temple and Small Temple) carved into rock. It was built by the celebrated pharaoh Ramesses II for himself and his wife Nefertari.

As the most elaborate Egyptian temple ever, **KARNAK** took an astonishing 2,000 years to build! It has the largest colonnaded hall, with columns that reach an impressive 75 feet in height.

Many mysteries still surround the **GREAT SPHINX OF GIZA** — the largest statue in the world carved from a single piece of rock. For example, how old is it? And what purpose did it serve? Scientists think that it was carved during the reign of Pharaoh Khafre (3rd millennium BCE) and that the face of the Sphinx is actually his likeness. The lion's body symbolizes the ruler's power.

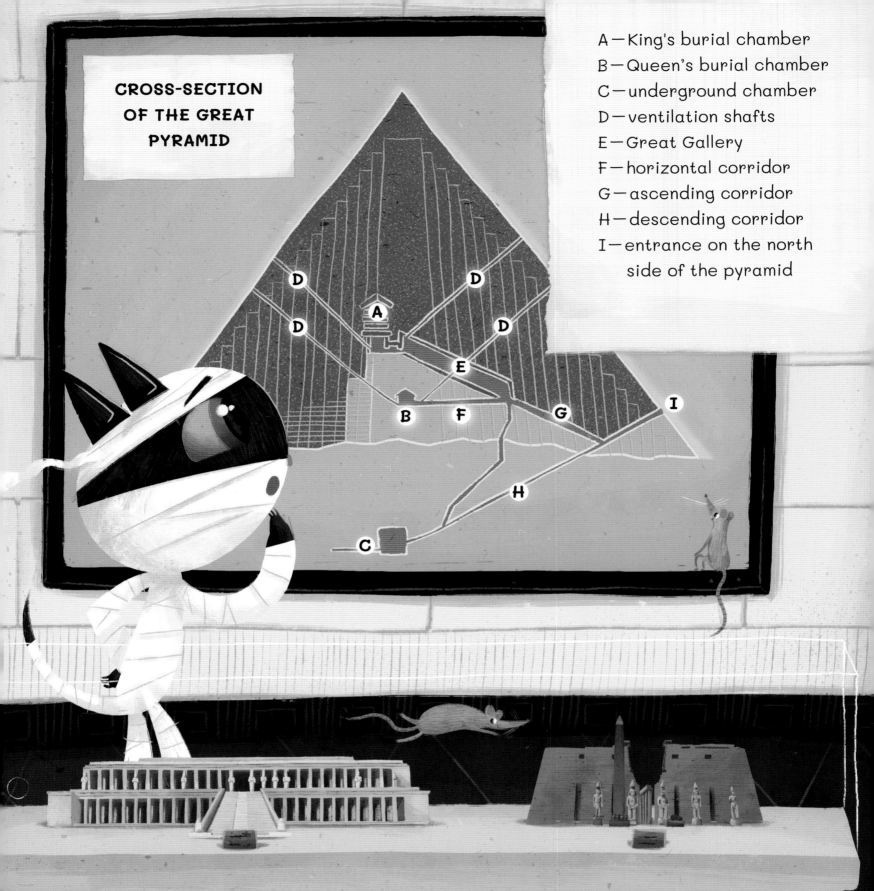

CROSS-SECTION OF THE GREAT PYRAMID

A — King's burial chamber
B — Queen's burial chamber
C — underground chamber
D — ventilation shafts
E — Great Gallery
F — horizontal corridor
G — ascending corridor
H — descending corridor
I — entrance on the north side of the pyramid

The monumental terraced **MORTUARY TEMPLE OF QUEEN HATSHEPSUT** is carved into white limestone rock. The construction of the temple, which in Egyptian was called the "Holy of Holies," took "only" 15 years.

The **TEMPLE COMPLEX IN LUXOR** is not as large as the one in Karnak, but it is no less important. Amenhotep III had it made, and it was dedicated to the god Amun. The palace of the temple complex is one of the oldest parts. There are also remarkable giant statues of the rulers called colossuses.

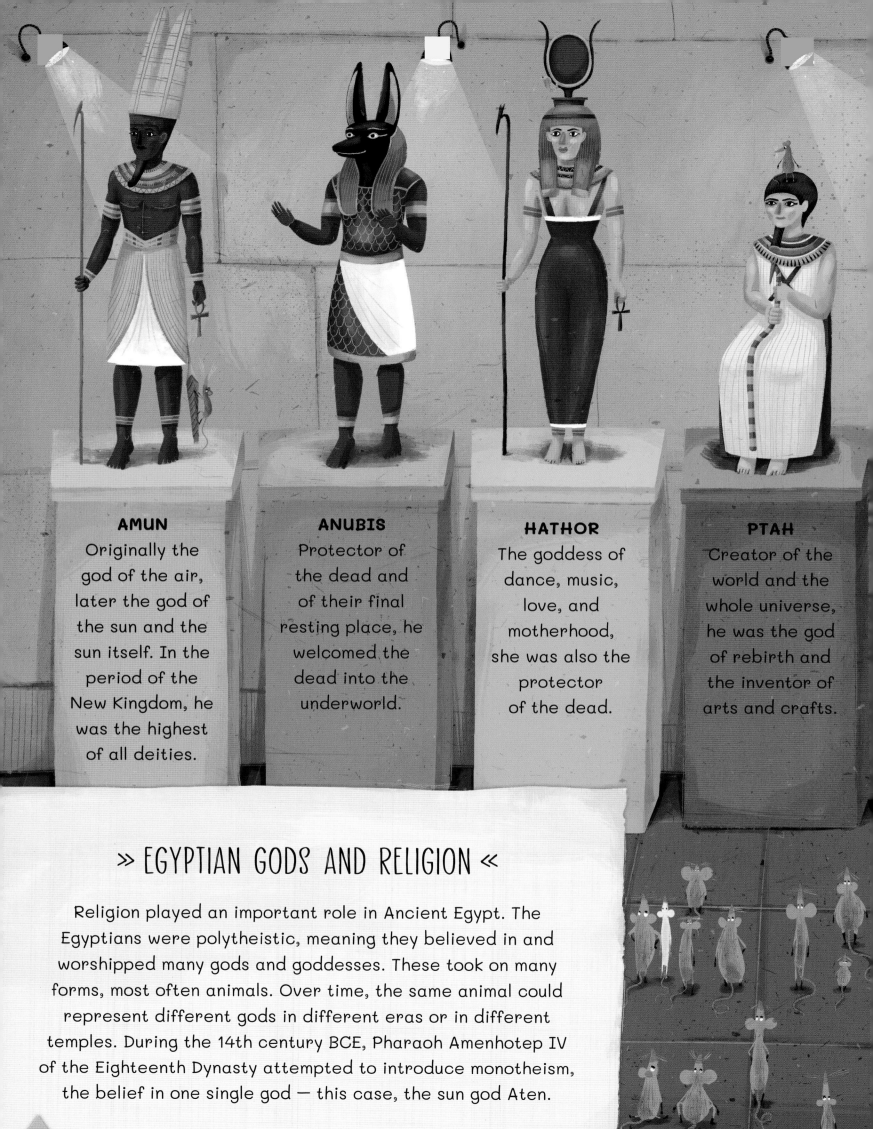

AMUN

Originally the god of the air, later the god of the sun and the sun itself. In the period of the New Kingdom, he was the highest of all deities.

ANUBIS

Protector of the dead and of their final resting place, he welcomed the dead into the underworld.

HATHOR

The goddess of dance, music, love, and motherhood, she was also the protector of the dead.

PTAH

Creator of the world and the whole universe, he was the god of rebirth and the inventor of arts and crafts.

≫ EGYPTIAN GODS AND RELIGION ≪

Religion played an important role in Ancient Egypt. The Egyptians were polytheistic, meaning they believed in and worshipped many gods and goddesses. These took on many forms, most often animals. Over time, the same animal could represent different gods in different eras or in different temples. During the 14th century BCE, Pharaoh Amenhotep IV of the Eighteenth Dynasty attempted to introduce monotheism, the belief in one single god — this case, the sun god Aten.

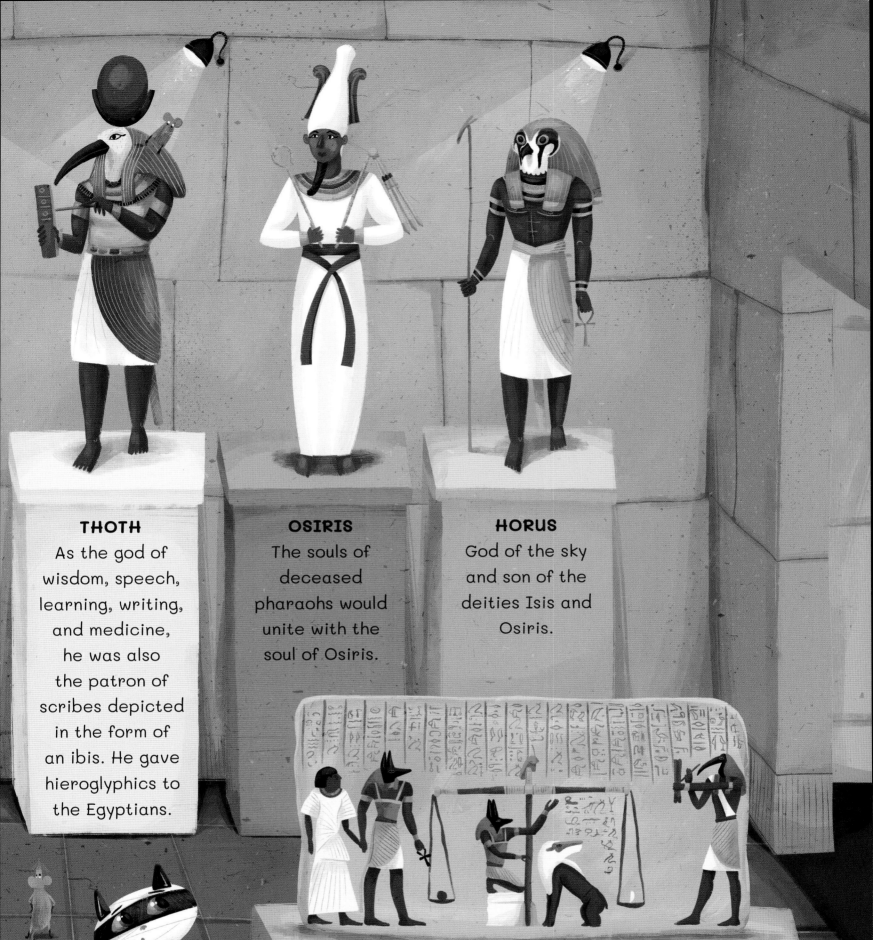

THOTH

As the god of wisdom, speech, learning, writing, and medicine, he was also the patron of scribes depicted in the form of an ibis. He gave hieroglyphics to the Egyptians.

OSIRIS

The souls of deceased pharaohs would unite with the soul of Osiris.

HORUS

God of the sky and son of the deities Isis and Osiris.

The **WEIGHING OF THE HEART** — This was done by the god Anubis and noted by the god Thoth. If the sinner's heart was heavier than a feather, the devourer of the dead Ammit would eat it. On the other hand, if the heart was lighter, it would pass through the gates of heaven and could begin to live in the afterlife.

LIFE IN EGYPT

If you think Ancient Egypt was a culture obsessed with death, then you are mistaken. It was quite the opposite, in fact. The Egyptians loved their lives and even believed that they were living the best life possible in the best of all possible worlds. See for yourself in our unique film.

THIS FILM WON THE GOLDEN SCARAB 2024 AWARD FOR BEST DOCUMENTARY!

One jump and I'm in a film!

HOUSES OF THE LOW BORN — Low-born Egyptians lived in dwellings made of sun-dried mud bricks. These dwellings had two or three rooms with small windows and a kitchen in a small yard. (The whole family lived in the rooms, including livestock animals) These houses had flat roofs, so the inhabitants could spend their leisure time on the roof. On hot nights, they even slept up there.

HOUSES OF THE WEALTHY — Wealthy Egyptians lived in large houses centered around a large hall illuminated by the sun. The central hall was surrounded by a bedroom, a toilet, and a bathroom (with a bath), while the kitchen was located in a small courtyard. The house stood in the middle of a well-kept garden, which included a swimming pool for cooling down.

In Ancient Egypt, women ran the household. They made sure the home was clean and had drinking water. Women, along with their children, looked after the family garden and the domestic animals. For noble women, these tasks, as well as bringing up the children, were done by servants and slaves. On the other hand, noble wives helped their husbands entertain foreign dignitaries.

Ancient Egyptian women had the same rights as men. They could own businesses, land, and homes. They could divorce on their own, enter into contracts with men, and use their property as they wished. There was no such equality anywhere else in the ancient world.

Ancient Egyptians were very happy when they had children. Mothers nursed their children up to the age of four. During that time, they were carefree and played with toys. After that, the children began helping their parents. Boys helped their fathers in their work and girls helped in the home and helped look after younger siblings. The children of noble families would receive an education.

The Egyptians were very keen on fashion. They took a particular interest in clothing and tried to keep up with the latest trends.

Women went from wearing skirts to a long slim dress with shoulder straps, which was called a kalasiris. Children wore no clothes until the age of ten.

In early times, men wore a short wraparound skirt, which was fastened at the waist with a fabric or leather belt. Later, they wore starched pinafores (an apron-like garment), pleated cloaks, or another skirt made of transparent material.

Most Egyptians walked barefoot or in ordinary reed sandals. Wealthy people wore sandals made of leather or painted wood.

Egyptians regularly used make-up to look more attractive. They believed that the more striking their make-up was, the greater the gods would favor them. So they lined their eyes with a thick black powder called kohl, which reached their temples, and they painted their eyelids with a green metallic color up to their eyebrows. The green color of the eyeshadow also protected their eyes from heat, wind, dust, and sand.

Ordinary Egyptians were mostly vegetarian. The foundation of their diet was bread and vegetables, dates, figs, onions, and sheep's milk. Meat was expensive, so they seldom ate it, except, for example, when they managed to catch a fish or a water bird.

The only sweetener of Ancient Egypt, which was highly prized, was honey. The Ancient Egyptians loved it so much they even cooked vegetables in it. No wonder the bee was a sacred insect in Ancient Egypt.

CHAIRS were originally intended for the ruler and only spread to wider society later.

These practical, lightweight and popular **STOOLS** had folding legs in the shape of an X.

The chairs of the pharaohs were intricately carved, inlaid with gold and ivory, and also had cushions and upholstery.

The chair legs were shaped like animal paws.

ORDINARY EGYPTIAN HOUSES WERE CERTAINLY NOT CLUTTERED WITH FURNITURE. Ancient Egyptians favored airy spaces and light compact furniture, so you wouldn't have come across any bulky wooden furniture. Rather, you'd find folding stools, couches, reed beds, cabinets, tables, and chests to store belongings. Wood was scarce in Ancient Egypt, so only the wealthiest could afford wooden furniture. In any case, the furniture in their homes was much cheaper in quality than the burial goods they took with them to the afterlife.

EGYPTIAN BEDS
were light wooden structures with straps attached to them. This way, cooling air could flow around the sleeper on hot nights.

BEDSIDE TABLES were an essential piece of furniture in Egyptian bedrooms. Containers with ointments and perfumes were placed on them.

PAINTED STORAGE chests were common among both rich and poor. They were made of wood, ivory, or reeds.

Slate sculpture of Pharoh Menkaure and his wife Khamerernebty II (circa 2515 BCE).

Limestone statue of a seated scribe at work — one of the most famous Egyptian sculptures, from 2620—2500 BCE.

Pharaoh Djoser sitting on the throne. The oldest statue of a pharaoh, it is 4.5 feet tall.

EGYPTIAN ART served a religious, social, and political function. As part of the cult of the pharaoh, it helped give immortality to the pharaoh and his family. All works of art were intended for the gods. They were a message for the deities, who were said to receive and read them. Statues were a big part of Egyptian buildings and architecture. Statues that were not in palaces, temples, or buildings would have seemed very out of place to the Egyptians of that time. Egyptian sculptors created sculptures that were both life-sized and monumental, with chiseled faces and realistic proportions. Overall, they were stiff yet majestic.

Painted statues of prince **Rahotep** and his wife **Nofret** (4th dynasty, 2580 BCE)

Sculpture of pharaoh Khafre (4th dynasty)

Was i as pretty as that? I, Nefertiti?

ANCIENT EGYPTIAN ARTISTS didn't use perspective in their paintings. Objects and figures that were meant to be far away were drawn towards the upper edge of the picture, while nearby objects were situated towards the lower edge. They attempted to depict the character or object as faithfully as possible and thus provide the viewer with as much information as possible. This is why the painters drew the bodies of the figures from the front but the heads in profile — that way, the observer could get a well-rounded idea of the figure. Likewise, the eye was drawn from the front, so that the white of the eye and its iris and pupil could be seen clearly. The legs and feet were again drawn in profile. The more important a person was, the more strictly this rule was observed.

Ancient Egyptian artists painted with brushes made of reed stalks, the ends of which they chewed into thin fibers.

COLOR SYMBOLISM

For Ancient Egyptians, blue symbolized night and the heavens. Light ochre was used for women's skin tone. Dark ochre was used for men's skin tone. Green symbolized youth.

Palm fiber brushes for spreading paint

The **EARLIEST INSCRIPTIONS** carved into stone or slate come from the Predynastic Period around 3000 BCE — that is, from the time before the rise of the united kingdom of Lower and Upper Egypt. Back then, the Sumerians, one of the oldest civilizations in the world, had a great influence on Egypt. They inspired the Egyptians to create their own script. And so they created a specific pictorial script called **HIEROGLYPHS**. No one outside the borders of the empire understood how to read them. Even within the empire, hieroglyphs were only used by the ruling class.

In **HIEROGLYPHIC WRITING**, words were written next to each other without spaces. It was possible to write them from left to right, from right to left, or from top to bottom. However, for better clarity, the individual letters were grouped into squares. The names of the pharaohs were written in oval frames called cartouches. Hieroglyphs were used only for religious and cult purposes.

HIEROGLYPHICS CONSISTED OF THREE TYPES OF SCRIPTS:

Pictograms—signs representing things, characters, and ideas
Phonograms—signs expressing sound
Determinatives—signs used to distinguish words that are spelled the same but have different meanings.

In addition to hieroglyphics, there was also a simplified form of writing in Egypt called **hieratic script**. Trained scribes used it to write everyday documents, such as recipes, account info, rhymes, and literary texts.
Hieratic script is as old as hieroglyphic script.

PAPYRUS — This was one of the main materials for writing on. It was made from the papyrus plant, which grew in abundance throughout the Nile Valley in Ancient Egyptian times.

The **ROSETTA STONE** was significant because it contained three identical texts written in Egyptian hieroglyphs, hieratic script, and Ancient Greek. Thanks to the Greek text, the 19th-century French linguist and archeologist Jean-François Champollion deciphered the Egyptian script.

Hey, not so fast, kitty cat! Come back! I want to tell you about the glorious year of 1822, when I, of all people - a poor French linguist and archeologist - solved the great mystery of the hieroglyphs.

SCRIBES were the only people in Ancient Egyptian society who could write hieroglyphs, which were their divine scripts. Because of their services, they didn't have to pay taxes or be in the military. Scribes were privileged in Egyptian society and were highly regarded. They worked in offices, warehouses, and ports. To learn to read and write, they had to study hard in temple schools, where they patiently practiced writing individual letters on pieces of papyrus or carving them on limestone tablets. They also learned to make their own pens, papyrus, and ink.

In Ancient Egypt, life was all about family and fun! Everyone spent their free time playing with their loved ones, participating in sports and games, and celebrating special occasions. Physical fitness was highly valued, and even the pharaohs exercised regularly. Children of the era had a wide variety of simple toys to choose from.

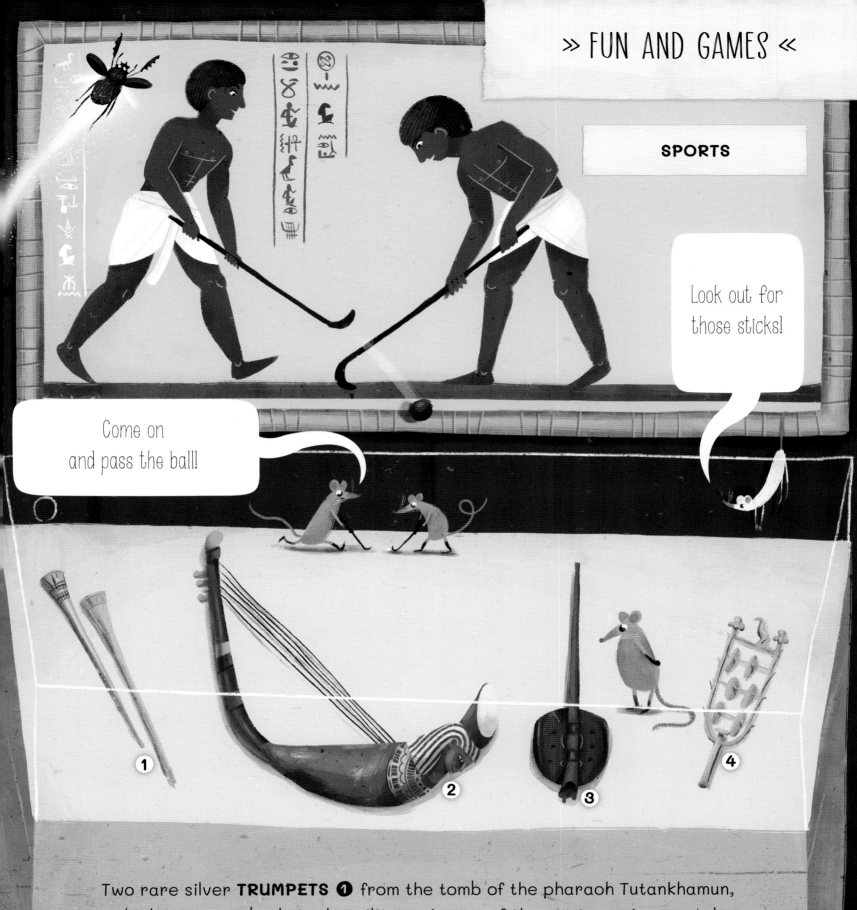

SPORTS

Look out for those sticks!

Come on and pass the ball!

Two rare silver **TRUMPETS** ❶ from the tomb of the pharaoh Tutankhamun, which were used only in the military. As one of the most precious metals in Ancient Egypt, silver was valued way more highly than gold. The Ancient Egyptian **HARP** ❷ had between 11 and 13 strings. In addition to large instruments like these, there were also smaller shoulder harps. The Ancient Egyptian **LUTE** ❸ was a string instrument, and the **SISTRUM** ❹ was a sacred rattle-like instrument used in religious ceremonies dedicated to the goddess Hathor.

SENET was one of the most popular Ancient Egyptian board games. The game represented the journey to the afterlife.

You have climbed the House of Water! Now you have to wait until you roll a 4 . . .

MEHEN — Another popular Ancient Egyptian board game, this one took the form of a coiled snake.

DOLLS ❶ — made from cloth, clay, and ceramics.
BALLS ❷ — made from old cloth or dried palm leaves wrapped in strips of animal hide.
HORSE ON WHEELS ❸ — a toy that is popular even today. **MILL FOR GRINDING GRAIN ❹**.
CERAMIC MOUSE ❺.

Don't mind me, sir . . .

BANQUETS — The Ancient Egyptians enjoyed banquets, where they ate, drank, played music, and danced. Professional dancers provided entertainment for all the guests, with men dancing with men and women dancing with women.

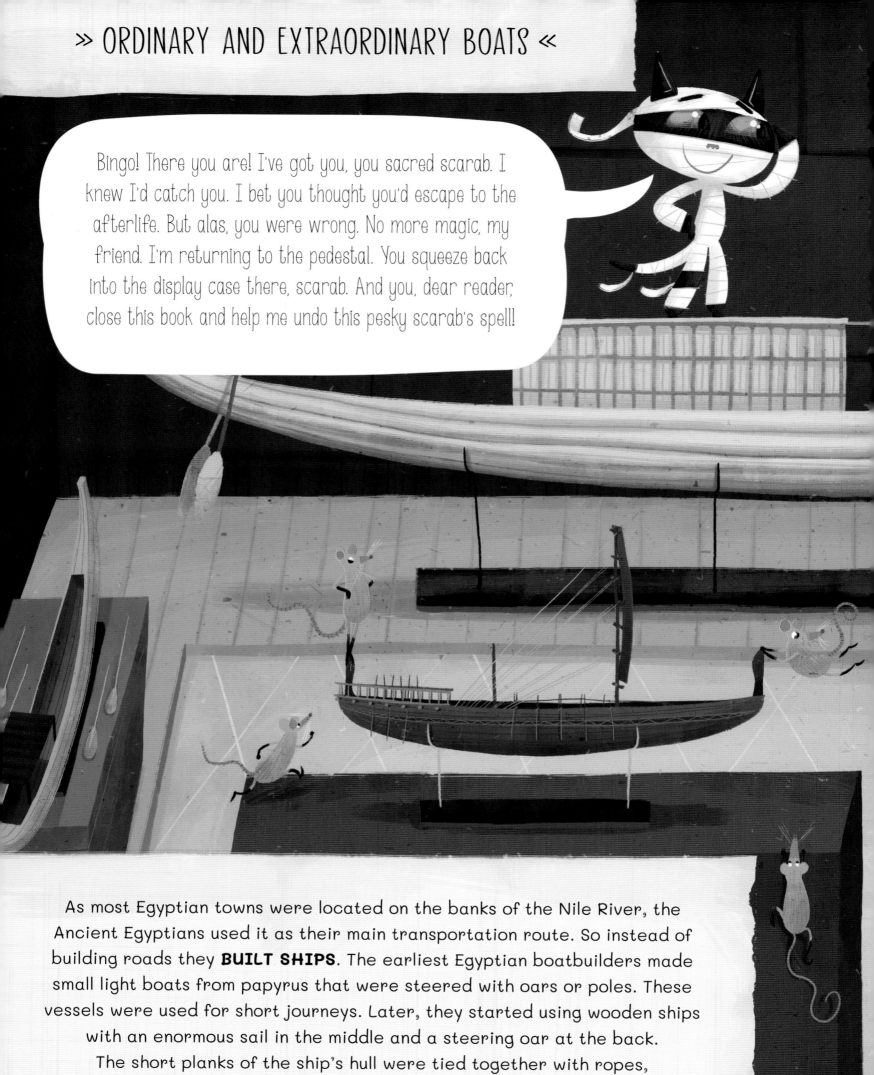

Bingo! There you are! I've got you, you sacred scarab. I knew I'd catch you. I bet you thought you'd escape to the afterlife. But alas, you were wrong. No more magic, my friend. I'm returning to the pedestal. You squeeze back into the display case there, scarab. And you, dear reader, close this book and help me undo this pesky scarab's spell!

As most Egyptian towns were located on the banks of the Nile River, the Ancient Egyptians used it as their main transportation route. So instead of building roads they **BUILT SHIPS**. The earliest Egyptian boatbuilders made small light boats from papyrus that were steered with oars or poles. These vessels were used for short journeys. Later, they started using wooden ships with an enormous sail in the middle and a steering oar at the back. The short planks of the ship's hull were tied together with ropes, as the Egyptians didn't use nails.

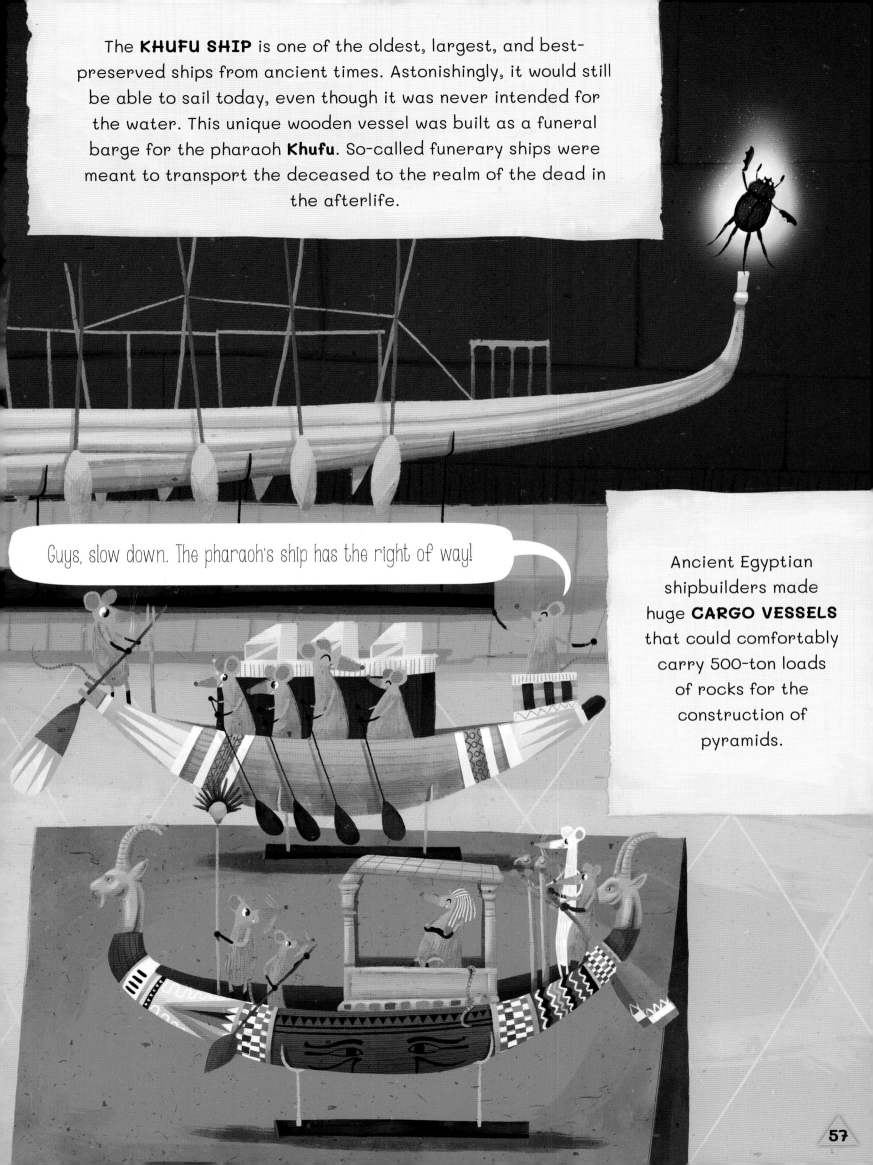

The **KHUFU SHIP** is one of the oldest, largest, and best-preserved ships from ancient times. Astonishingly, it would still be able to sail today, even though it was never intended for the water. This unique wooden vessel was built as a funeral barge for the pharaoh **Khufu**. So-called funerary ships were meant to transport the deceased to the realm of the dead in the afterlife.

Guys, slow down. The pharaoh's ship has the right of way!

Ancient Egyptian shipbuilders made huge **CARGO VESSELS** that could comfortably carry 500-ton loads of rocks for the construction of pyramids.

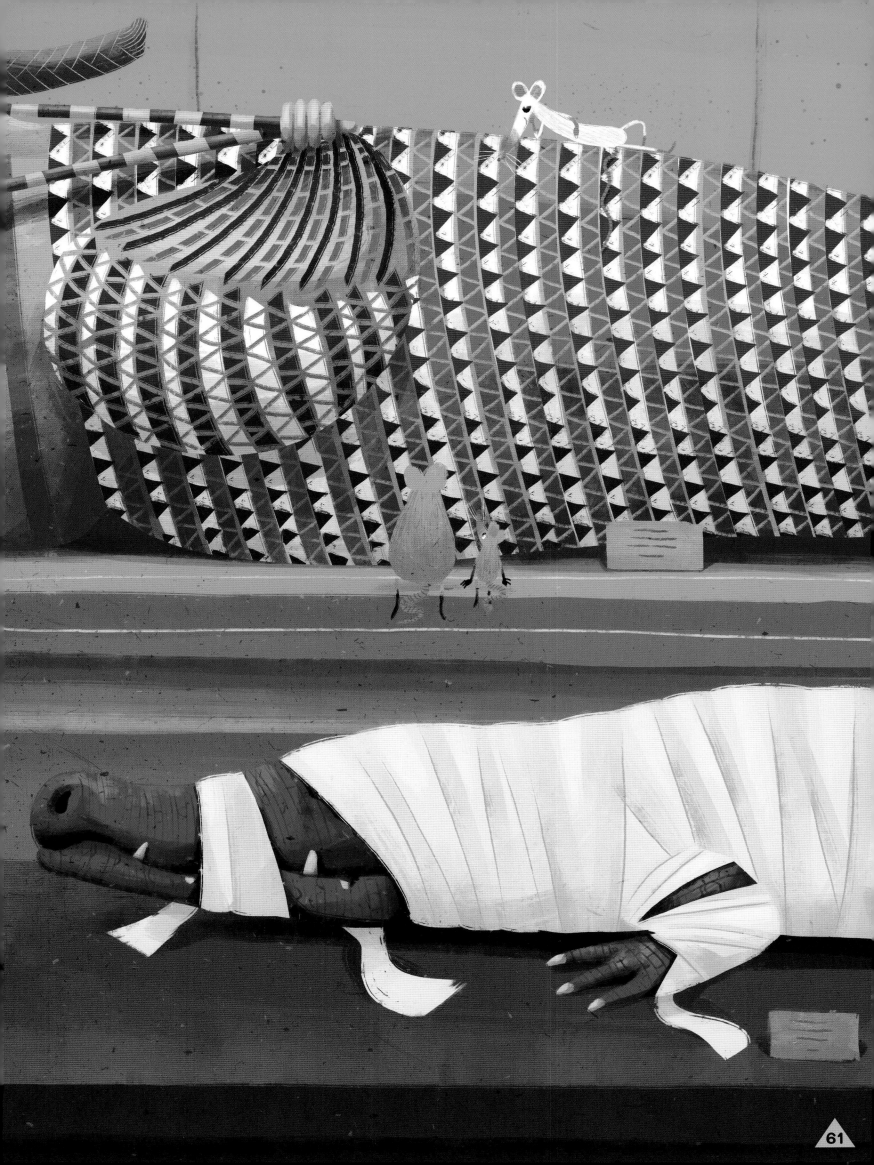

» GLOSSARY «

A

Ankh — an Egyptian cross symbolizing life.

Aristocrat — a member of the nobility.

B

Banquet — a social event where people eat, drink, dance, and play musical instruments. They were very popular in Ancient Egypt.

C

Canopic jars — containers in which the internal organs of the dead were stored.

Carter, Howard — the amateur archeologist who discovered the virtually untouched tomb of the previously insignificant pharaoh Tutankhamun.

Champollion, Jean-François — French linguist and archeologist who deciphered Egyptian hieroglyphs.

D

Determinatives — hieroglyphic characters used to distinguish words that are spelled the same.

H

Hierarchical proportion — a type of painting where more important or higher status people were painted larger and taller than less important people.

Hieratic script — a simple script designed for writing secular documents (recipes, accounts, and literary texts).

Hieroglyphs — typical Egyptian pictorial script used for writing religious and cult texts.

K

Kalasiris — a slim dress with straps worn by Ancient Egyptian women.

M

Mehen — a popular Ancient Egyptian board game in the form of a coiled snake.

Mummification workshops — houses of purification, places where the Egyptian dead were mummified.

N

Nemes — a striped headdress worn only by Egyptian rulers, worn in place of a crown.

Nubian wood — wood imported from Nubia in southern Egypt, usually ebony.

P

Papyrus — the primary material for writing on in Ancient Egypt, made from the stems and pith of the papyrus plant.

Pectoral — the decorative collar of the pharaoh, the jewelry worn on their chest.

Pharaoh — the title of rulers of Ancient Egypt.

Phonograms — hieroglyphic characters expressing sound.

Pictograms — hieroglyphic signs representing things, ideas, or figures.

R

Rosetta Stone — a stone slab with inscriptions in three different scripts: hieroglyphic, hieratic, and Ancient Greek. Its discovery helped scholars decipher Egyptian hieroglyphs.

S

Sarcophagus — a box in which a coffin was placed, usually made of stone.

Scarabaeus sacer (*sacred scarab*) — a beetle from the scarab family that for the Ancient Egyptians was a symbol of reincarnation and the cycle of life. Amulets in the form of scarabs were placed on the hearts of mummies.

Senet — a popular Ancient Egyptian board game.

Sistrum — a rattle-like musical instrument that was sacred.

U

Ushabtis — figurines of helpers that were meant to serve the deceased in the afterlife. They were commonly found among the burial goods of the deceased.

V

Vizier — the the highest ancient Egyptian official, a representative of the pharaoh.

PLEASE DON'T WAKE UP OUR SACRED SCARABS!

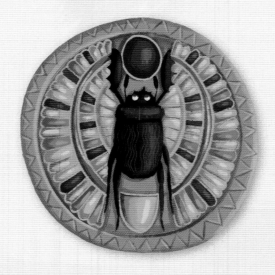

Scan the QR code for more
information and sources.

MAGICAL MUSEUM:

ANCIENT EGYPT

© B4U Publishing for Albatros,
an imprint of Albatros Media Group, 2024
5. května 1746/22, Prague 4, Czech Republic
Written by Štěpánka Sekaninová
Illustrations © Jakub Cenkl 2023
Translated by Mark Worthington
Edited by Scott Alexander Jones

www.albatrosbooks.com

Printed in China by Leo Paper Group